PROCESS IMPROVEMENT FOR ADMINISTRATIVE DEPARTMENTS

THE KEY TO ACHIEVING INTERNAL CUSTOMER SATISFACTION

By Willie L. Carter

ISBN: 1-4392-0104-8
ISBN-13: 9781439201046

Visit www.booksurge.com to order additional copies.

CONTENTS

PREFACE

Many times organizations overlook the importance of collaboration and communication between their administrative departments. Work is completed by one department and "thrown over the wall" to the other department with total disregard for the needs or requirements of the department to whom the work is handed off.

With this type of mindset poor quality documents, information, and data leads to rework and wasted time which ultimately impacts the delivery of services or products to the external customer—"the one who pays the bills."

Administrative departments need to create a new mindset in which they view downstream departments as their customers because they truly are their internal customers. This approach is remarkably evident if you think of the work you do as a process. In process thinking you receive an input from a supplier which you transform into a product or service for your downstream customer. Your goal as the processor department is to make sure your downstream customer is satisfied every single time.

This handbook is designed to provide you, the reader, with proven real world tools and techniques to improve your work processes and thereby satisfy your internal customers. The methodology in the handbook represents a systematic approach to process improvement. It gives administrative teams a practical model and set of tools for analyzing and redesigning their work.

I can vouch for the effectiveness of these tools and techniques because I have used them throughout my career to help organizations make their administrative processes more effective and more sensitive to their internal customers' needs. I've also found that when an organization does a good job of satisfying internal customers that they do a much better job of satisfying their external customers.

Finally, I suggest you change your perspective and start to look at tasks as a related series of events—a process, and embrace the tools and techniques in this handbook to make your administrative departments more effective in meeting the requirements of their customers. The benefits to the organization are more robust, waste-free, flexible processes designed to achieve higher levels of customer satisfaction.

Willie L. Carter

SECTION 1

INTRODUCTION

Purpose of this Handbook

This handbook offers a proven method for going about managing and improving natural work group or department level quality. The fundamental premise is that all work is a process which converts an input to an output for a customer. The intent of this handbook is to help the reader or practitioner satisfy the organization's internal customers, which ultimately leads to satisfaction of the external customers.

The driving force for developing this handbook was the recognition of the need for a structured approach to managing and improving the quality and processes of administrative departments. However the underlying principles are applicable to any department.

Benefits of the Methodology

The disciplined application of the entire methodology leads to sustained improvement in department level processes. Benefits include:

- Reduced fire-fighting

- Better collaboration between the major work groups within the organization

- Clarification of work priorities

- Systematic identification and removal of the root cause of problems

- Fact-based decision making

- Prevention of problems

Using the Handbook

This is a book of guidelines not rules. The handbook is a roadmap for achieving internal customer satisfaction. To realize the benefits of the handbook the guidelines must be applied with sound management judgment and adapted to fit your organization.

The steps in improving an administrative department's process quality basically follow the Plan-Do-Check-Act (PDCA) continuous improvement cycle. The first eight steps make up the **Plan** phase of the PDCA cycle, step nine is the **Do** phase, step ten is the **Check** phase, and step eleven is the **Act** phase of the cycle.

SECTION 2

The Fundamentals

Definitions

As used in this handbook:

Customer—the recipient or beneficiary of the outputs of the process work efforts or the purchaser of its products or services. The customer may be internal or external to the organization.

Input—the information, materials, and resources required to create products or services.

Output—the product, information, or service provided to another individual or work group.

Process—a set of interrelated work activities characterized by a set of specific inputs and value-added tasks that produce a set of specific outputs.

Process performance—refers to how effectively and efficiently a process satisfies customer requirements.

Quality—meeting or exceeding customer expectations every single time.

Supplier—the individuals or groups who provide inputs to the process. Suppliers can be internal or external to a company, group, or organization.

Processes and Systems

There is a tendency to think of your organization as a place where numerous tasks are accomplished; putting labels on envelopes, stamping letters, calling customers, and on and on. Process management challenges us to look at these tasks in a different light, to think of them as steps in a process. Precisely how did the stamp get on the envelope? Where did the envelope come from and how did it get there?

We can define a process by grouping in sequence all the activities or tasks directed at accomplishing one particular result. For example, the steps in hiring or training a new employee or the steps in entering an order are part of a process. Taken in this context we begin to see that every activity is part of a process, and there are many processes in every organization.

A whole new perspective opens up when you begin to see tasks as a related series of events. You begin to understand the interrelationship between departments throughout the organization. It helps you focus your thinking because realizing that the organization works through processes, you can only improve your work by improving your processes.

What Is Process Improvement?

You can delight your customers by providing the "best" possible products or services. Best is defined as meeting or exceeding your customers' expectations.

You can only provide the "best" product or service by improving the processes that produces them. You do not improve a process by weeding out the good from the defects and errors after a product or service is produced. Instead process improvement is about improving quality, while reducing costs and eliminating waste.

Process improvement typically means making a process more efficient, less costly, more capable of meeting your customers' requirements, and/or more consistent in producing a value-added output for the customer.

Customers and Suppliers

The concept of customers and suppliers is easily grasped once you understand the idea of a process: the people or departments who precede the series of tasks you identify as a process are "suppliers" and those who follow, who use the product or service, are "customers." These definitions include customers and suppliers both inside ("internal") and outside ("external") the organization.

External customers buy the product, financially supporting the organization; therefore it is important to satisfy these people. Inside the company, employees pass on their work to other employees, who are their internal customers.

Each employee therefore is a *customer* of preceding employees; and each has *customers,* the people to whom the employee passes his or her work.

You cannot focus solely on the product from the process or the person delivering the service and still be able to deliver quality to your customers. Process excellence is determined by the quality of the inputs and how well each step of the process is performed. Therefore, you must build quality into every step, process, and system in the organization. You must work with internal and external customers to determine their needs, and work in partnership with internal and external suppliers.

The Quality Responsibilities of Every Department

Customer Responsibilities	Processor Responsibilities	Supplier Responsibilities
Convey needs to suppliers	Design and plan the process to meet customer needs	Identify your customers
Give feedback to suppliers	Manage the process to meet customer needs	Be aware of customer needs
Acquire feedback from suppliers	Improve the process based on customer feedback & requirements	Acquire feedback from customers

Process Complexity

The root causes of a problem is sometimes hidden deeply in the procedures and processes used to create a product or service. But even when the original source is hidden, you can usually find the non-value-added activities that were generated in compensating for the problem. These non-value-added activities are complexities—something that makes a process more complicated without adding value to the product or service.

Typically, complexity arises when people repeatedly try to improve a process without an organized plan. Then try to solve one piece by adding or rearranging steps, without realizing they are altering other parts of the process. As the problems from the alteration start to surface, more and more steps are added to compensate. Almost every process includes work that would not be necessary if systems worked perfectly.

The Four Types of Process Complexity

- Errors/Defects—when defects occur in products or services, or an error is made, work has to be repeated and extra steps added to correct the error or dispose of the damage. These steps are complexity because they are non-value-added in the eyes of the customer.

- Delays—when work is waiting for approvals, information or others to complete a task

- Waste—The use of more material, time and movement than absolutely necessary

- Variation—disparity in work output typically caused by doing things differently. The lack of standardized methods for completing the work routinely causes variation.

SECTION 3

The Steps to Process Improvement

Step 1: Define the Mission of the Department

The department should develop a mission statement. The mission statement describes the department's work clearly, concisely, and concretely. It says what the department does and defines why the department exists? The statement should be brief (25-30 words), relevant, and easily understood by everyone in the department. It should be customer-oriented, focusing on the products and services provided. The mission statement lays the foundation for everything that follows. If done well it provides direction and a sense of purpose for the entire department. It should focus on the primary reason for the department's existence. e.g., *to produce accurate expense checks for our customers on a timely basis.*

It is extremely important that all members of a department participate in developing the mission statement because it creates ownership and facilitates achievement of the mission. Some sample mission statements are shown below.

Examples of Department Mission Statements
Production Department

"To manufacture and ship defect free product for our customers on time."

Purchasing Department

"To provide quality raw materials for our customers on time at the most efficient cost."

Quality Control Department

"To provide accurate and timely test results for our customers."

Finance Department

"To provide accurate and timely financial reports for our customers."

R & D Department

"To provide technical support and reliable products for our customers in a precise and prompt fashion."

Step 2: Determine the Work Products (Outputs) of the Department

Output is the product, service, or information the department provides to a person or another work group.

Develop a brainstormed list of all activities carried out by the department. The question to ask is, "What does the customer receive from this process?" Products may include documents, data, or information. Services may include training, information processing, and maintenance. Reviewing the list, identify the critical activities – those that are most closely related to achieving the department's mission. The critical activities are then examined to define the principal products or services created as a result of these activities.

Two useful tools for determining and ranking your work products are brainstorming and multi-voting

Tools

🕑 *Brainstorming*

🕑 *Multi-voting*

Brainstorming is a process by which a group of people create a "storm of ideas". It works best when the entire group participates. There are two major methods for brainstorming:

1. *Structured. A process in which each team member gives ideas in turn.*

2. *Unstructured. A process in which team members give ideas as they come to mind.*

I have found the structured approach to provide more discipline within a group; therefore I will list the steps for that approach.

Structured Brainstorming

1. **The central brainstorming question is stated, agreed upon, and written down on a flipchart.**
   Make sure everyone understands the issue or problem. Validate this by asking one or two members to restate it before writing it down on the flipchart.

2. **Each team member, in turn, gives an idea without criticism.**
   As you rotate around the team, any member can pass at any time.

3. **Write each idea in large visible letters on a flipchart.**
   Make sure the ideas are recorded in the exact words of the speaker, don't interpret or abbreviate.

4. **Ideas are generated in turn until each person passes, indicating that the group has exhausted all possible ideas.**

   Keep the process moving and relatively short—5 to 30 minutes works well depending on the complexity of the topic.

5. **Review the list of ideas for clarity and to discard any duplicates.**

   Discard only ideas that are virtually identical preserving subtle differences in slightly different wordings.

Multi-voting is a way to conduct a poll or vote to select the most important ideas from the brainstormed list.

1. **First brainstorm a list of ideas and number each one.**

2. **With agreement from the group combine similar items and discard duplicate ideas.**

3. **If necessary renumber the remaining ideas.**

4. **Have all members of the group choose several ideas they would like to discuss or address by writing the numbers of those ideas on a sheet of paper.**

   Allow each member a number of choices equal to at least one-third of the ideas on the list. For example if there are 15 ideas on the list each member is allowed to choose 5 of the ideas.

5. **After all members have silently completed their selections, tally the votes**

   You may let members vote by a show of hands as each idea is called out.

6. **Reduce the list by eliminating those ideas with the fewest votes**

   A rule of thumb is: Small group (5 or fewer) cross off the ideas with 1 to 2 votes, medium sized group (6 to 15), eliminate anything with 3 or fewer votes, large group (more than 15) eliminates ideas with 4 or fewer votes.

7. **Repeats steps 3 through 6 for the remaining list with the choices reduced accordingly. Continue this until the top 3 to 5 ideas remain**

Step 3: List in Priority Order all Products and Services

The products or services created are then prioritized relative to the department's mission. The result should be a prioritized list of products or services, produced by the department closely related to the mission. Flowchart the internal work process for the vital few activities and major products and services.

The flowchart is a great tool for graphically displaying your process.

Tool

⏱ *Flowcharting*

The flowchart allows a team to identify the actual flow or sequence of events in a process.

Steps (Refer to exhibits 1 and 2)

1. **Determine the boundaries of the process.**
   Define where the process starts (input) and ends (final output).

2. **Determine the steps in the process.**
   Brainstorm a list of all major activities, inputs, outputs, and decisions on a flipchart from the beginning of the process to the end.

3. **Sequence the steps.**
   Using 2" by 3" sticky notes arrange the steps in the order they are carried out. Sticky notes allow the team to move the steps around if necessary.

4. **Draw the flowchart using the appropriate symbols (see exhibit 1 for a list of flowchart symbols).**

5. **Test the flowchart for accuracy.**
   Validate the flowchart with people who are not on the team and who carry out the process. Make sure every feedback loop is closed.

6. **Finalize the flowchart**
   Make sure the flowchart actually depicts the process—are employees following the process as charted? Look at ways to eliminate non-valued-added tasks or redundancies.

Basic Flowchart Symbols

Symbol	Represents	Detail/Example
(rounded rectangle)	Terminator: Start/End Input/output	Request for proposal, request for new hire, raw material
(rectangle)	Task, action, execution point	Hold a meeting, make a phone call, open a box
(diamond, No / Yes)	Decision point	Yes/no Accept/reject Pass/fail Criteria met/not met
(document shape)	Document	A report or form is filled out, job request, meeting minutes
(delay shape)	Delay	Waiting for service, report sitting on a desk
(circle with A, arrow)	Continuation	Go to another page, go to another part of the chart
(arrow)	Arrow	Shows direction or flow of the process steps

Exhibit 1

Flowchart Example

Completing a Check Request

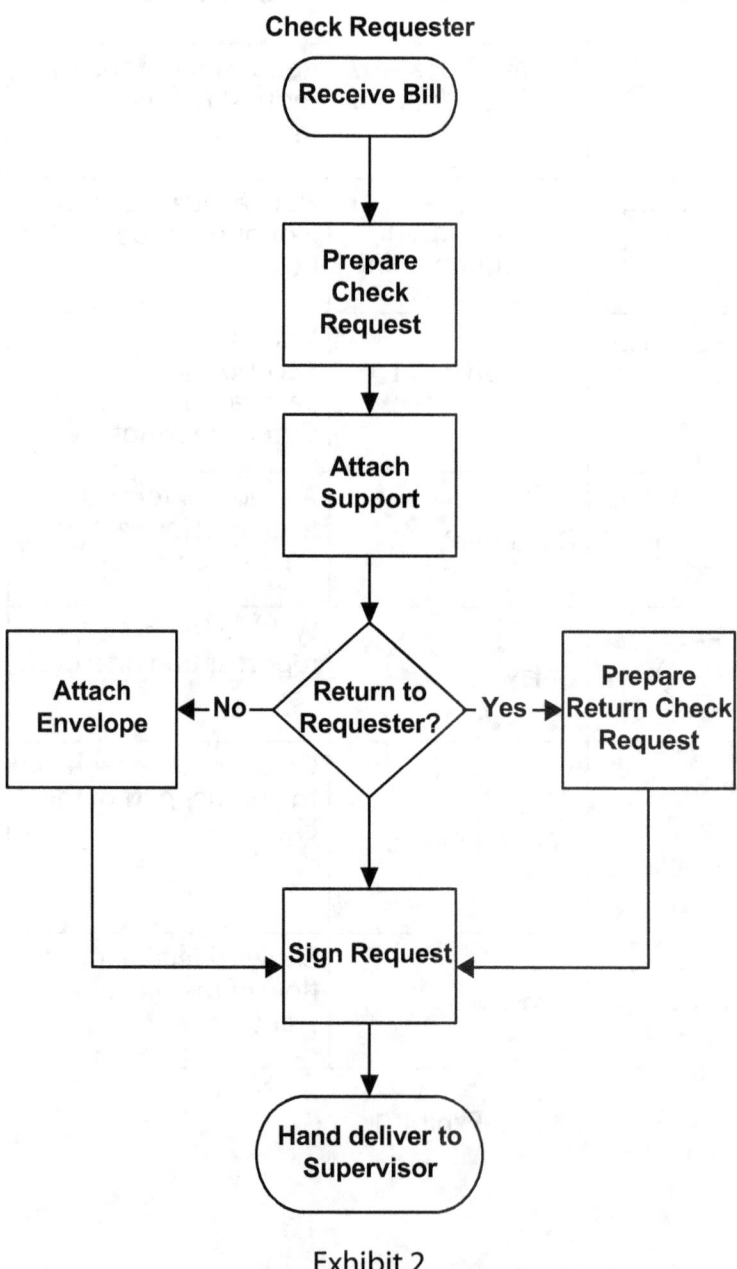

Exhibit 2

Step 4: Identify and List the Vital Few Customers of Your Priority Products

List the internal and external customers who receive the prioritized products in. In most cases a department's customers will be internal. Examples of possible customers are:

- *Internal*—individual, work group, or department to whom you give work, products, services, or information within the same organization

- *External*—is anyone outside the organization who receives its products, services, or knowledge. Commonly the ultimate paying customer, although government agencies and regulatory bodies are included

Not everyone has contact with an external customer, but nearly every department does something that is ultimately seen outside the organization.

Most departments have a long list of customers. The group should narrow down this list to the vital few customers and plan to contact each one of them. In most cases the vital few customers are the people or groups significantly impacted by the department's activities—department supervisors and key employees within the customer unit.

The department's activities may also impact some of the useful many customers and the group may need to identify selected categories of those internal customers. The customer- supplier sundial and the supplier-input-process-output-customer (SIPOC) chart are two useful tools that can help you identify your customers and your priority products.

Tools

- ⏱ *Customer-Supplier Sundial*

- ⏱ *SIPOC Chart*

The customer-supplier Sundial is a graphic tool the department can use to identify the vital few customers of its priority products.

Steps (Refer to exhibits 3–6)

1. **The team starts the sundial exercise by inserting the name of the department in the center circle of the sundial.**

2. **The department then inserts its vital few customers in the spokes of the sundial.**

3. **Choosing one of the spokes to focus on the team determines the product or services it provides to that customer.**

The Customer-Supplier Sundial

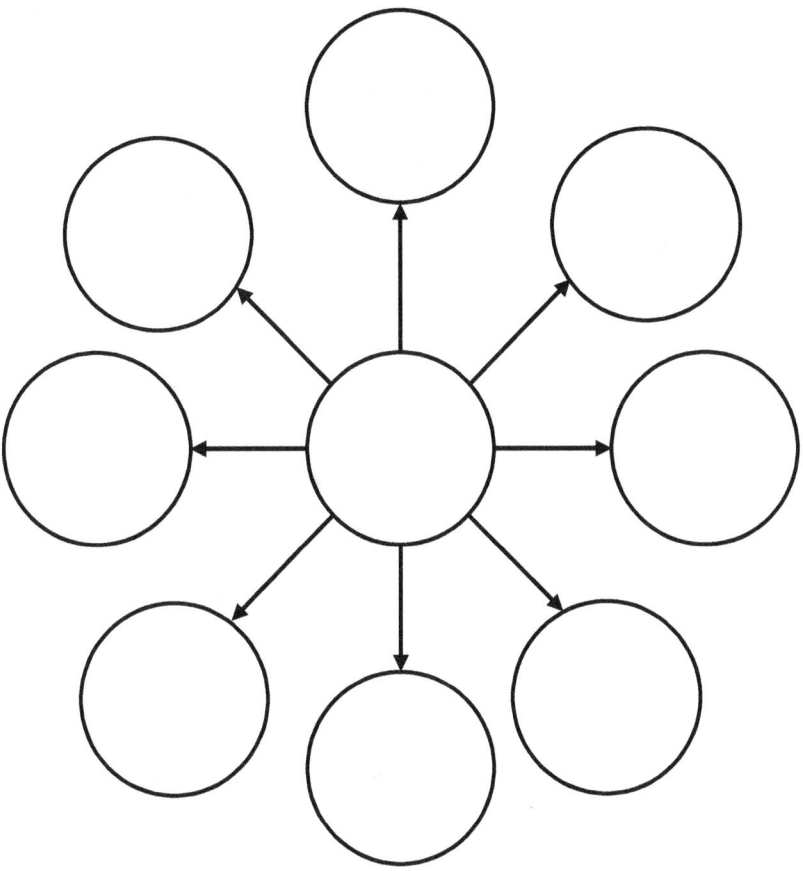

Exhibit 3

The Customer-Supplier Sundial

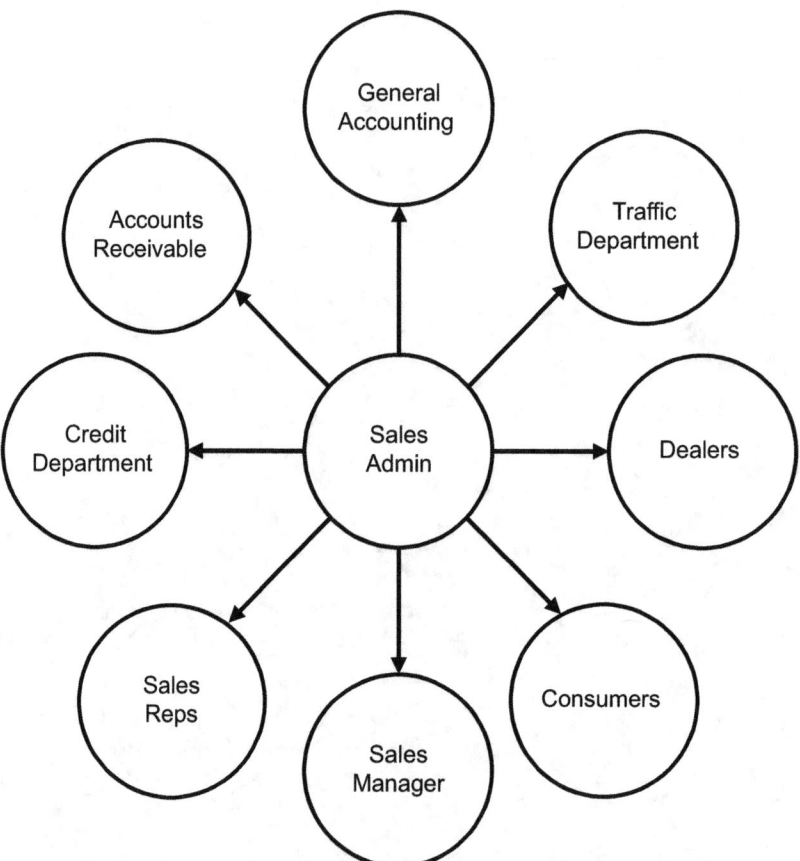

Exhibit 4- Customers of a Sales Administration department

A Spoke from the Sundial

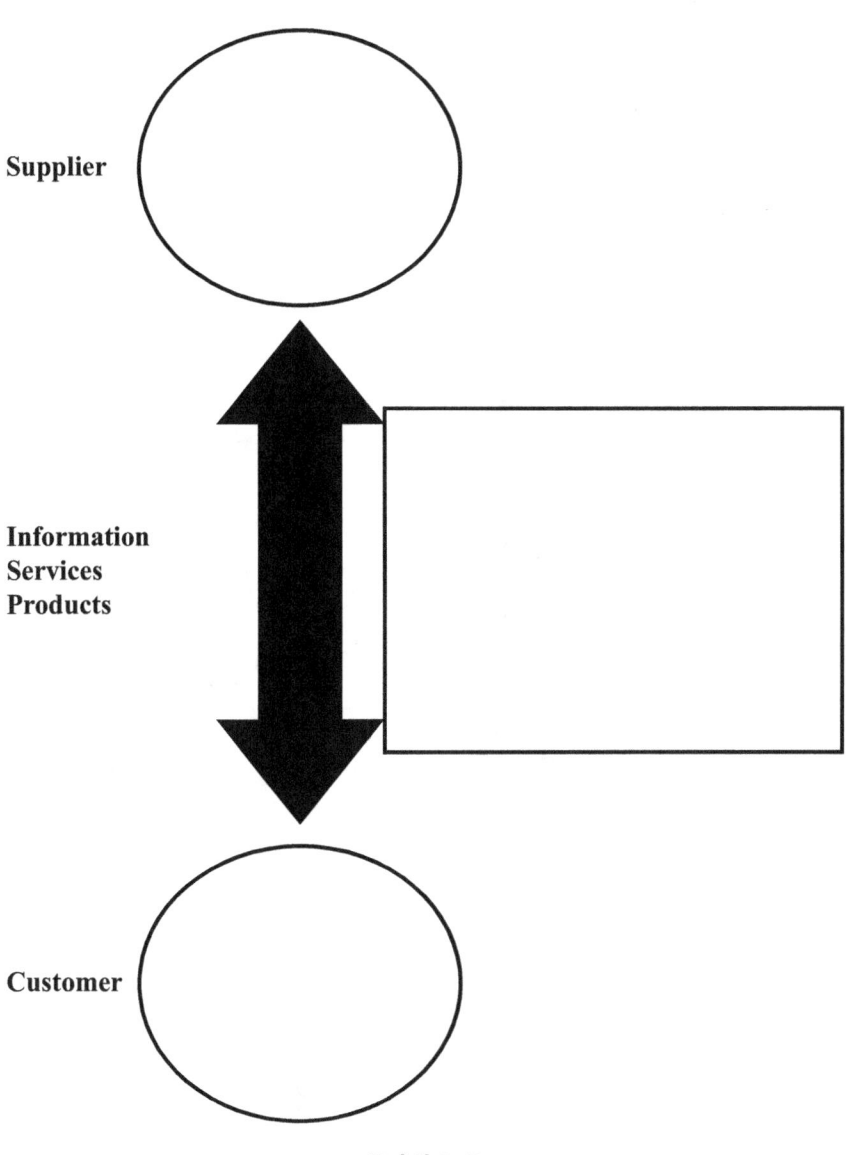

Exhibit 5

A Spoke from the Sundial Example: The major products provided by the Sales Administration department to its major customer, the credit department.

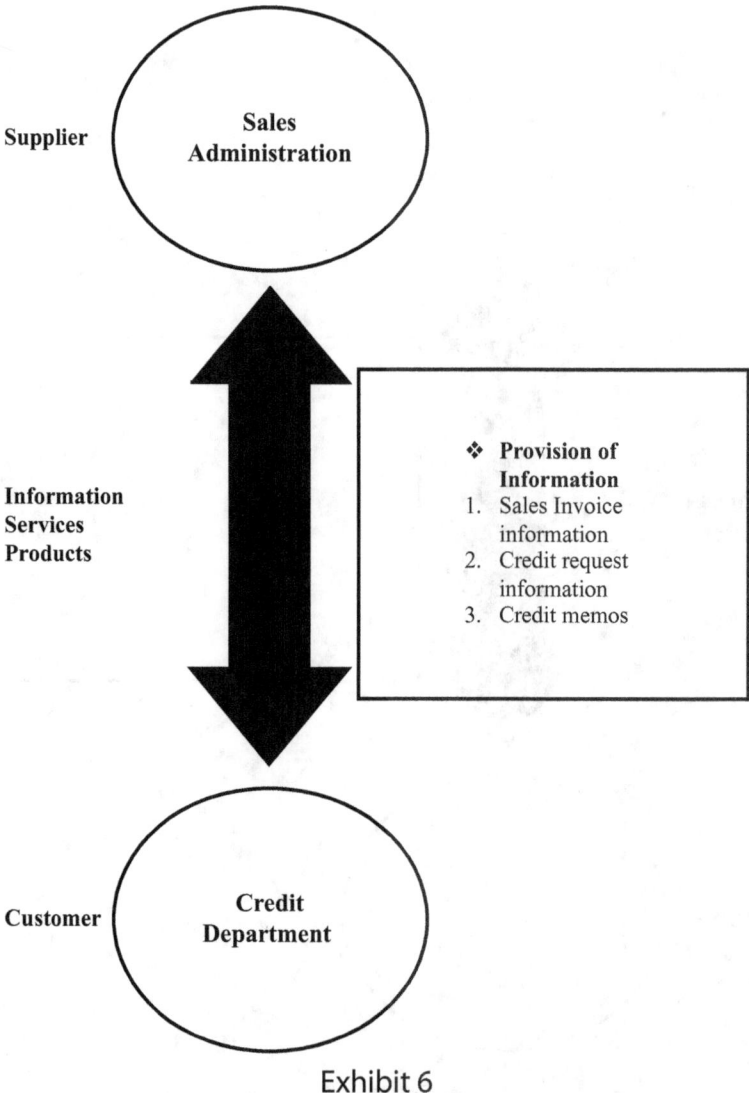

Exhibit 6

The SIPOC chart is another tool the department team can use to identify its vital few customers as well as the suppliers, inputs and outputs of the process.

Steps (Refer to exhibits 7 and 8)

1. **Identify the suppliers of the input and list them in the first column.**

2. **Identify the inputs provided by the suppliers and list them in the second column.**

3. **Determine what the department does to convert the inputs to outputs (the process) and list them in column three.**

4. **Identify the outputs from the process and list them in column four.**

5. **Determine the customers of the output and list them in column five.**

There is no set order to completing the columns. A team can start with step five first and work backwards through the matrix. A department could list the processes first and then complete the matrix randomly.

SIPOC Chart—Suppliers—Inputs—Process—Outputs—Customers

Your Department: _____

SIPOC

Suppliers	Inputs	Process	Outputs	Customers
Supplies your inputs	*Products or services that enter unit boundaries*	*What you do to convert inputs to outputs*	*Products or services that exit unit boundaries*	*Receive products or services that exit unit*

Exhibit 7

SIPOC Example

Your Department: Sales Administration

SIPOC

Suppliers	Inputs	Process	Outputs	Customers
Supplies your inputs	*Products or services that enter unit boundaries*	*What you do to convert inputs to outputs*	*Products or services that exit unit boundaries*	*Receive products or services that exit unit*
Sales Customers	Purchase Order	Processing Orders	Bills of lading Invoices	Credit department Traffic department
Credit Dept	Debit memos	Debit verification	Credit information	Credit department
Dealer	Complaint	RGA	RGA number	Sales Reps Dealers
Sales Reps	Purchase Orders	Order processing	Invoices	Accounts receivables

Exhibit 8

Step 5: Identify Customer Requirements and Express them from the Customer's Viewpoint

The definition of quality is meeting or exceeding the customer's requirements every single time. Interview your customers to determine their requirements of the product or service in question. Some basic methods for gathering information are:

1.   Customer interviews

2.   Customer audits/questionnaires

3.   Customer focus groups

4.   Surveys

For internal customers usually conducting interviews will provide sufficient information regarding their requirements.

Understanding customer requirements is a critical first step in process improvement. Clarity up-front in the process means that the time is taken early on to learn about the customer and to understand their unique needs. Clearly defining requirements is the key to managing your process and establishing your scope of service. Planning and agreement early on prevents rework later on in the process. Perhaps, more than any other single variable, meeting customer requirements guarantees customer satisfaction and a relationship of mutual trust between your department and internal customers.

Customer requirements are the driving force behind process improvement. You need to understand how your customers use your output and engage them in dialogue to determine their needs.

Functional analysis matrices and customer needs tables are very useful and simple tools to help you confirm and rank your customers' needs and see how they compare to what you believe the needs are.

Tools

- ⏱ *Functional Analysis*
- ⏱ *Customer Needs table*

Steps (Refer to exhibits 9 and 10)

1. **Select one major customer from the SIPOC or Sundial exercise.**

2. **Select an important product or service from the SIPOC or Sundial chart.**

3. **List the customer needs associated with that product or service and rate the relative importance of the needs. The weighting should total to 10 points.**

4. **Set up a meeting with your customer. Let them know the purpose of the exercise and the product or service that you would like to work on.**

5. **Ask your customer to select those needs, which are important to them (compare the differences between the needs selected by your customer and yourself).**

6. **Have the customer select the top 3 or 4 needs and weigh them by relative importance (a total of 10 points).**

7. **Independently the supplier (department) and the customer should rate the past performance for each need using a scale of 0 to 10, with 0 being total failure to meet the need and 10 being total success in meeting the need.**

8. **Multiply the weight factor by the score for each need to get a total performance rating (a perfect total rating is 100).**

9. **Compare the differences in the rating with the customer. Use the low customer perceived ratings and the areas with large supplier-customer discrepancies to identify opportunities.**

10. **Identify measures by which you can determine customer satisfaction (the supplier should focus on process measures and the customer should focus on outcome measures).**

Functional Analysis Summary Sheet

Supplier:

Customer:

Product or Service:

Supplier Evaluation Grid

Customer Needs					*Total*
Weight Factor					**10**
Supplier Score					
Weight X Score					

Customer Evaluation Grid

Customer Needs					*Total*
Weight Factor					**10**
Customer Score					
Weight X Score					

Exhibit 9

Example

Functional Analysis Summary Sheet

Supplier: Sales Administration
Customer: Traffic Department
Product or Service: Bills of lading

Supplier Evaluation Grid

Customer Needs	Timely	Accurate	Complete		*Total*
Weight Factor	4.0	5.0	1.0		**10**
Supplier Score	7.0	8.0	9.0		
Weight X Score	**28.0**	**40.0**	**9.0**		**77.0**

Customer Evaluation Grid

Customer Needs	Timely	Accurate	Complete		*Total*
Weight Factor	2.0	4.0	4.0		**10**
Customer Score	5.0	8.0	8.0		
Weight X Score	**10.0**	**32.0**	**32.0**		**74.0**

Exhibit 10 – Functional Analysis for the Sales Administration Department

(Note: Although there isn't a big difference between the supplier and customer total score, notice the difference between the customer and supplier scores on completeness. The customer believes completeness is far more important than the supplier thought—this is an opportunity for improvement.)

🕐 *Customer Needs Table*

This is another simple tool a team can use to determine and rank customer needs. It consists of a matrix in which the defined customer needs are ranked in importance from 1 to 5.

Steps (Refer to Exhibits 11 and 12)

1. **Determine the quality attributes associated with your process and output (for example, timeliness, accuracy, completeness) and enter them under customer needs. (You may need customer input to determine attributes).**

2. **Ask a representative set of customers to rank order the list of customer needs.**

3. **Use the customer needs table to tally the results. For each box multiply the number of strokes times the rank. Then add the score for each line.**

4. **The lower the score the higher the priority to the customer.**

Customer Needs Table

Rank

Customer Needs	1	2	3	4	5	Total	Final Rank

Exhibit 11

Customer Needs Table

Example

Rank

Customer Needs	1	2	3	4	5	Total	Final Rank
Timeliness	// 2×1=2	/// 3×2=6	/// 3×3=9	// 2×4=8		25	2
Accuracy	///// 5×1=5	/// 6	// 6	0		17	☆ 1
Completeness	/ 1×1=1	// 4	/// 9	//// 16		30	4
Courtesy	// 2×1=2	// 4	// 6	//// 16		28	3

Exhibit 12

Step 6: Translate Customer Needs to Department's Language

The customer's requirements must be translated into a language the provider department can understand. A key question to ask is: If our customers say they need this, how can we go about providing it?

How do we translate the requirement into the department's language? Many times customers speak in concepts. You need to convert those concepts to a measurable objective—in other words you will need to obtain an operational definition. An operational definition is something you and the customer can conduct business with. For example, many times an internal customer will say the report has to be "timely." What does timely mean? To you, timely could mean delivering the report 5 days after month-end close, but could mean 2 days after month-end close to the customer. We need to have the customer operationally define "timely" so that there is mutual agreement on the objective.

Your department may be unable to meet the customer's needs at the onset, but your goal should be to establish a plan to meet them in the future.

Two tools you can use to determine customer and supplier requirements are the customer requirements and supplier requirements tables.

Tools

🕐 *Customer Requirements Table*

🕐 *Supplier Requirements Table*

A simple matrix used to translate customer or supplier requirements into measures and track process performance.

Steps (Refer to exhibits 13–16)

1. **For each output, list the associated key quality characteristic, units of measure, and performance targets (customer and supplier requirements).**

2. **Record actual process performance.**

(Note: The measures determined with the customer/supplier requirements tables are the quality metrics for step 7. Based on your customer's expectations, go back to your supplier and negotiate your requirements and feedback mechanisms. See exhibit 14.)

Customer Requirements Table

Customer: _____

	Output	Quality Characteristic	Unit of Measure	Performance Target	Actual Performance
Customer Requirement # 1					
Customer Requirement # 2					
Customer Requirement # 3					
Customer Requirement # 4					

Exhibit 13

Supplier Requirements Table

Supplier: _____

	Output	Quality Characteristic	Unit of Measure	Performance Target	Actual Performance
Supplier Requirement # 1					
Supplier Requirement # 2					
Supplier Requirement #3					
Supplier Requirement #					

Exhibit 14

Customer Requirements Table Example

Customer: Controller

	Output	Quality Characteristic	Unit of Measure	Performance Target	Actual Performance
Customer Requirement #1	Financial Report	Accuracy	Number Of Errors	0 errors	5 errors
Customer Requirement #2	Financial Report	Timeliness	End to end Processing Time in Days	3 days	4 days
Customer Requirement #3					
Customer Requirement #4					

Exhibit 15

Supplier Requirements Table Example

Supplier: General Accounting

	Output	Quality Characteristic	Unit of Measure	Performance Target	Actual Performance
Supplier Requirement #1	**Journal Entries**	Timeliness	Time Document Submitted	Before 10 am Wednesday after close	2 pm Wednesday after close
Supplier Requirement #2	**Journal Entries**	Accuracy	Number of Errors	100% error free	85% accurate
Supplier Requirement #3					
Supplier Requirement #4					

Exhibit 16

Step 7: Establish Quality and Process Metrics

Establish a set of measures. These measures (metrics) will help continuously monitor how well the department is conforming to the customer's requirements. A quality metric is simply a statement of what will be measured – it should be specific. Some examples of quality metrics are:

1. The number of items to the customer with errors or defects per week.

2. The number of items delivered to the customer.

3. The number of customer complaints received per month.

4. The number of days required fixing errors or defects.

Measures are important because they provide data that will help your department to identify and solve problems. They are also central to defining a problem, and understanding how to solve it. Measures are important indicators of the health of the process.

List any measures you are currently collecting and evaluate them for; reflecting the voice of the customer and their capability of measuring and tracking each critical customer expectation; their effectiveness in helping you manage your process to deliver what the customers want; and finally, ensure that your existing measures encourages the department's team to meet customer requirements.

Look for alternative measures that cover what the existing measures miss. Evaluate the alternatives by the same criteria used to judge your existing measures.

This exercise will yield a list of current and possible measures that can help you provide what the customers want. In all likelihood the list will be too long to be practical. You will have to select the vital few measures that you need to improve your process and satisfy your customers.

The quality measures should refer to numbers not percentages. Percentages sometimes create a false sense of security. Unless the percent of improvement is a "Big Hairy Audacious Goal", like a 50% reduction in error rate, they don't stimulate action to improve. It is also useful to revisit the flowchart of step 3 and establish process indicators that measure the effectiveness and efficiency of key intra-departmental transactions. That is, how well are two groups in the same department meeting each other's needs?

More often than not you will need to improve your process to meet your customer requirements, which means, you will have to establish process measures. There are three fundamental types of process measures: customer, producer and supplier measures.

Customer or result measures are used to ascertain the outcome of your process. They tell you how well your process is doing to meet customer requirements. For example, let's say you are a member of the Sales Administration Department in our earlier SIPOC example. Your measures of a quality bill of lading is that it is processed and delivered to the Traffic group on time and that the information is accurate even though there might be some missing shipment information. However, the Traffic Department's measures of a quality bill of lading are that when they receive it the information is accurate and that the bill of lading includes all the items to be shipped (complete). The Traffic group is not overly concerned so much about how fast you deliver it to them. If you are interested in satisfying your customer, you should be measuring and tracking accuracy and completeness of the bills of lading.

Producer or in-process measures lets you know how well your process is performing at certain critical points in the process. In-process measures keep your process in control and also make it more predictable. Back to the bill of lading example, you've learned that the Traffic department values accuracy and completeness. So the in-process elements of your bills of lading process that you should be measuring are things like the quality of the information needed to complete the bill and the accuracy of the inventory records stored on the computer.

Supplier or input measures help you assess how well your suppliers are meeting your requirements. These measures are typically established independently with each supplier to your process. Let's return to the bill of lading example. You are dependent on other departments (suppliers) to provide you with quality information on a timely basis so you can fully satisfy the Traffic Department. Therefore you need to measure the quality of the information and accuracy of the inventory records you use to create the bills.

Step 8: Establish a Plan to Meet Customers' Requirements

This step completes the plan part of the Plan-Do-Check-Act (PDCA) cycle within the department level improvement process. This step includes collecting the input from the previous seven steps and creating a department plan. The plan should be brief, customer focused, and biased for action. It should outline key actions the department expects to take based on its process quality planning work to date, and it should include goals for the metrics established earlier i.e., *fewer than five errors per month.*

One way to help determine the key actions for the department is to develop a flowchart or process map of your process and analyze it for complexity. Identify the non-value-added activities that prevent you from achieving your established goals—activities that can be eliminated from the process. Over time processes become more complex. This complexity leads to inefficiencies because it consumes more time and accomplishes less.

Revisit the flowchart in step 3 and examine each activity, decision and arrow on the flowchart (they represent time and effort). From the customer's perspective very little of this time and effort adds value, much of it is non-value-added. You can deliver error free products/services faster to your customers by simplifying the overall process—eliminating non-valued-added activities.

A very simple way to analyze a process is to create a checklist and for each arrow, activity and decision step on your flowchart, list its function and the time spent. Step into your customer's shoes and ask the following questions:

- Is the inspection, checking, or approval necessary?
- Is the step or activity redundant or can it be combined with other steps?
- Is the service or product delayed?

If the answer to any of these questions is "yes" then the step may not add value. If so we must determine how to remove it from the process. Some examples of non-value-added activities in administrative departments includes documents waiting in in-boxes or electronic mail boxes, making extra copies, excessive signatures or approvals, searching for computer files, unnecessary filing, repetitive data entry, and data entry errors.

In order to improve our processes so we can satisfy our internal customers, we must ask ourselves:

- How can non-valued added activities and delays be eliminated, minimized, combined or simplified to provide faster, higher quality flow through the process?

- How do we eliminate delays and prevent lost, changed, or misinterpreted information or work products at the hand-off points in the process?

After identifying the improvements make a commitment to implement them.

In addition the department level plan should also be designed to support key organizational goals. Any special process improvement projects in support of an organizational objective or critical success factor should be listed in the department plan. Everyone in the department should sign the plan, and it should be updated as necessary, at the very least quarterly.

Step 9: Implement the Plan

Now it is time to put the plan and knowledge into action. It is important that the entire department agrees to implement the plan. The supervisor of the department must take an intense interest in encouraging department employees to put the plan in action.

I recommend that you implement the identified improvements on a small scale or trial basis. The key activities involved in implementing process improvements on a small scale include:

- Root cause analysis of process problems—if you can identify the root causes of your process problems you can focus your improvement efforts with laser like precision

- Identify and prioritize improvement opportunities to streamline and modify your process—redesign the process to be more robust by eliminating non-value-added steps

- Select the best solutions for achieving your improvement goals based on your improvement criteria keeping in mind the impact on your customers

- Test your solutions on a small scale—do not make them standard procedure right away—experiment to determine how well they work

- Collect data on all key process measures—gather evidence to support or refute your improvement efforts

Step 10: Evaluate the Results

The department should continuously check on how it is doing by:

1. Monitoring its quality and process metrics.

2. Frequently surveying its customers and asking them how the department is doing?

These two methods of checking will reveal plan deficiencies, and keeps the department in touch with its customers so that it can build a positive relationship with them and quickly respond to any changing circumstances which may suggest a need to modify the plan.

Your goal in improving your process is to satisfy your customers, to make sure your improvement effort is working give it the acid test. Ask your customers. If your customers feel the effort is unsuccessful you may have to go back to the drawing board. If your customers concur that improvement has occurred then you are on the right track.

One way to obtain feedback is to conduct a customer satisfaction audit. The customer satisfaction audit is a proactive tool. This means that your department reaches out to the customers of your process to measure their satisfaction instead of waiting for them to complain about your services. See appendix A for an example of a satisfaction audit for administrative departments.

Step 11: Use Customer Feedback to Improve the Plan

The feedback from step 10 must be acted upon to modify the plan and actions to meet customer requirements. Two problems may occur from time to time. The simple "low hanging fruit" problems that the department can pounce on quickly and fix; or the chronic deep-rooted problems that will require assigning an improvement team to investigate.

In order to improve the plan the department will have to engage in solving some of the problems surfaced from customer feedback. There are many problem solving models but the model I've found to work best for administrative teams is the seven step model based on the same PDCA cycle we used to improve our administrative processes.

The Seven Step Problem Solving Model

1. **Define the problem**—based on feedback from your customers write a problem statement and assemble a team to solve the problem. Some useful tools for this step are Pareto analysis and the run chart.

2. **Describe the current process**—graphically display your process using the flowchart tool mentioned earlier.

3. **Identify and verify root causes**—construct a cause and effect diagram to identify the root causes and collect data to verify that they are the root causes. Brainstorming causes is very useful in this step.

4. **Develop a solution and action plan**—generate and rank the potential solutions also generate an action plan. Some useful tools for this step include the affinity diagram, responsibility matrix and Gantt charts.

5. **Implement the solution**—put your action plan in place and monitor the team's progress.

6. **Review and evaluate**—review the outcomes of the change, revise the process if required, standardize the improvement and continue to monitor the process. Some useful tools in this step include: run charts and Pareto analysis.

7. **Reflect on the learnings**—take the opportunity to contemplate what you learned and how it could be applied or adapted to other areas.

See Appendix C for a description of some of the improvement tools mentioned above.

Closing Words

Continual process improvement is a practical and powerful way to promote and maintain quality in your organization. By fully understanding the impacts and consequences of your activities, you can determine if your way of doing things is the best way to serve your internal and external customers.

Process improvement allows your staff, as part of a team, to understand and shape their work, to see its inherent worth as part of the entire organization. It allows your staff to collaborate with others to develop the best known way to do the work and meet their customers' requirements.

When people are encouraged to improve their work processes they gladly seize the opportunity to change their work situation and deliver a quality product or service inside and outside the organization.

References

AT &T Quality Steering Committee, (1988), *Process Quality Management & Improvement Guidelines*, New Jersey, AT&T Bell Laboratories Publication Center.

Capezio Peter, Morehouse Debra (1993), *Taking the Mystery Out Of TQM, A Practical Guide to Total Quality Management*, Hawthorne, NJ, Career Press.

Dexter Corporation (1992), *Dexstar TQM Program,* Hartford, CT.

Goal/QPC (2000), The Problem Solving Memory Jogger, Salem, NH.

Juran, Joseph M., Godfrey, Blanton A. (1999). *Juran's Quality Handbook*, Fifth Edition, New York, McGraw Hill.

Juran, Joseph M. (1988), *Juran On Planning For Quality*, New York, The Free Press.

Tague, Nancy R. (1995), *The Quality Toolbox*, Milwaukee, WI, ASQ Quality Press.

Appendix A

Customer Driven Satisfaction Audit

Customer Driven Satisfaction Audit

Customer: _____

1. With regard to timeliness of response from our department, what are your expectations?

2. With regard to accuracy of paperwork from our department, what are your expectations?

3. With regard to the condition of our product or service, what are your expectations?

4. With regard to the availability of our product or service, what are your expectations?

5. With regard to courtesy of service from our department, what are your expectations?

6. With regard to completeness of work from our department, what are your expectations?

7. With regard to helping you meet your cost objectives from our department, what are your expectations

Our Performance

Customer: _____

Please rate our performance on a scale of 1-10, with 10 being "we are totally meeting your expectations every single time" and 1 being "we are never meeting your expectations."

1. How would you rate department in meeting your expectations in regard to timeliness of response? Score: ____

2. How would you rate our department in meeting your expectations in regards to accuracy of paperwork? Score: _____

3. How would you rate our department in regards to the condition of our paperwork or information? Score: _____

4. How would you rate our department in meeting your expectations in regards to the availability of our product/service? Score: _____

5. How would you rate our department in meeting your expectations in regard to the courtesy of our service? Score: _____

6. How would you rate our department in meeting your expectations in regards to the completeness of our work? Score: _____

7. How would you rate our department in meeting your expectations in regards to achieving your cost objectives? Score: _____

Total Score: _____

Suggestions for Improvement

Customer: _____

1. What specific suggestions do you have for improving our timeliness of response?

2. What specific suggestions do you have for improving the accuracy of our paperwork?

3. What specific suggestions do you have for improving the condition of our paperwork?

4. What specific suggestions do you have for improving the availability of our product/service?

5. What specific suggestions do you have for improving the courtesy of our service?

6. What specific suggestions do you have for improving the completeness of our work?

7. What specific suggestions do you have for helping meet or reduce your costs?

Appendix B

Process Improvement Forms

The Customer-Supplier Sundial

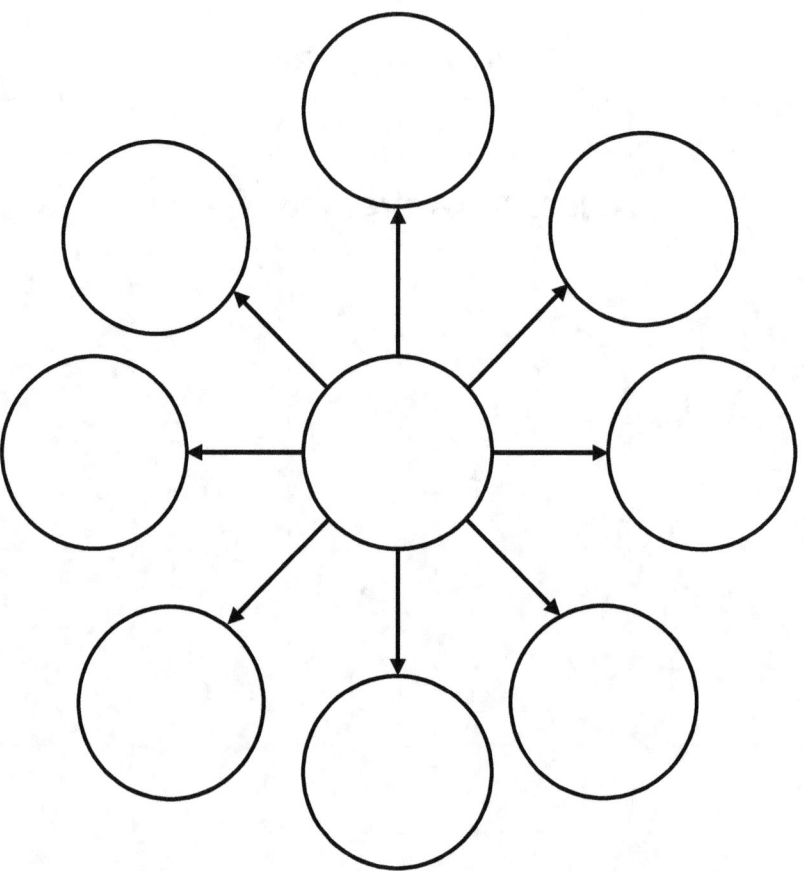

A Spoke from the Sundial

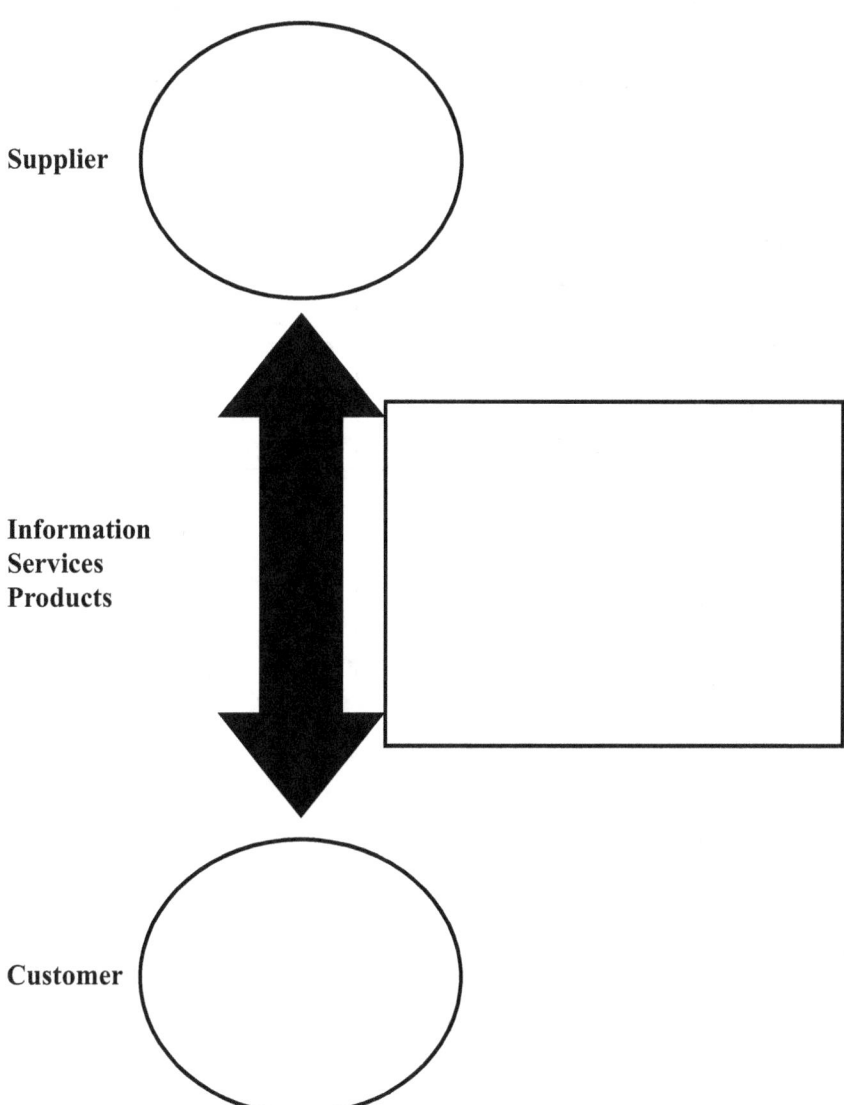

SIPOC Chart—Suppliers—Inputs—Process—Outputs—Customers

Your Department: _____

SIPOC

Suppliers	Inputs	Process	Outputs	Customers
Supplies your inputs	*Products or services that enter unit boundaries*	*What you do to convert inputs to outputs*	*Products or services that exit unit boundaries*	*Receive products or services that exit unit*

Functional Analysis Summary Sheet

Supplier:

Customer:

Product or Service:

Supplier Evaluation Grid

Customer Needs					*Total*
Weight Factor					**10**
Supplier Score					
Weight X Score					

Customer Evaluation Grid

Customer Needs					*Total*
Weight Factor					**10**
Customer Score					
Weight X Score					

Customer Needs Table
Rank

Customer Needs	1	2	3	4	5	Total	Final Rank

Supplier Requirements Table

Supplier: _____

	Output	Quality Characteristic	Unit of Measure	Performance Target	Actual Performance
Supplier Requirement # 1					
Supplier *Requirement* # 2					
Supplier Requirement # 3					
Supplier Requirement # 4					

Customer Requirements Table

Customer: _____

	Output	Quality Characteristic	Unit of Measure	Performance Target	Actual Performance
Customer Requirement					
Customer *Requirement*					
Customer Requirement					
Customer Requirement					

Appendix C

Additional Process Improvement Tools

Affinity Diagram

The affinity diagram organizes large numbers of ideas into their natural relationships. This tool taps into a team's creativity and intuition.

Used when:

- Issues seem to large and complex to grasp

- A breakthrough in new ideas is desired

- Group consensus is necessary

- Often used following a brainstorming session

Process

1. Record each idea with marking pens on a separate sticky note or card. Randomly spread notes on a table or wall so all or visible to everyone.

2. Team members gather around the sticky notes and without talking, place ideas that are related side by side. This is repeated until all cards are grouped. It is OK to have loners that don't seem to fit the groupings. It is alright to move a card someone else has already moved. If a card seems to belong to another group, make a second card.

3. Team members can talk during this step. When ideas are grouped, choose a heading for each group. Look for a card in each grouping that captures the meaning of the group. Place it at the top of the group. If there is no such card, write one.

Fishbone (Cause and Effect) Diagram

The fishbone diagram relates causes and effects. It can be used to structure a brainstorming session. It immediately sorts ideas into useful categories.

Used when:

- Broad thinking about potential causes is desired.

- When the team has reach an impasse in their thinking.

Process:

1. Agree on a problem statement (effect).

2. Brainstorm the major categories or causes of the problem. Generic headings like Methods, Machines, People, Materials, Measurement and Environment can be used if the team can't come up with their own categories.

3. Write the problem statement on a flipchart at the center right and draw a box around it. Draw a horizontal arrow running to the box. Write the categories or causes as branches to the main arrow.

4. Brainstorm all the possible causes of the problem, Ask "Why does this happen?" As each idea is given the facilitator writes it as a sub-cause branching from the appropriate main cause. Sub-causes can be written in several places if there are multiple relationships.

5. Ask again, "Why does this happen?" about each sub-cause. Write sub-sub-causes branching off the sub-causes. Continue to ask "Why?" and generate deeper level of causes. Layers of branches indicate causal relationships.

Pareto Chart

A Pareto chart is a bar graph. The bars represent frequency of occurrence or cost. Therefore the chart visually shows which situations are more significant.

Used when:

- Analyzing data by groups.

- Trying to focus on the most significant problem or cause.

- Communicating with others about your data.

- Relating cause and effect, by comparing a Pareto chart classified by causes with one classified by effects.

- Evaluating improvement, by comparing before and after data.

Process:

1. Decide what categories to use to group the items.

2. Decide what period of time the chart will cover.

3. Decide what measurement to use—frequency, percent, cost, time, quantity.

4. Collect the data.

5. Determine the appropriate number scale for the chart. Mark the scale on the chart.

6. Construct and label bars for each category. Place the tallest at the top far left, then the next tallest, and so on. If there are many categories with small measurements, they can be grouped as "other."

7. Calculate the percentage for each category: the total for that category divided by the total for all categories. Label each bar with its percentage, or draw a right vertical axis and label it with percentages.

8. Calculate and draw cumulative values: add the measurements for the first and second categories and place a dot above the second bar indicating the value, continue this process for all the bars and connect the dots starting at the top of the first bar. The last dot should reach 100% on the right vertical scale.

Matrix Diagram

The matrix diagram graphically shows the relationship between, two, three, or four groups of information. At the same time, it can show the relationship between the groups of information.

Used when:

- Trying to understand how one group of items relates to another group.

- Communicating how one group of items relates to another group.

- Allocating responsibilities among a group of people.

- Relating customer requirements to elements of a process.

Process:

1. Decide what group of items must be compared.

2. Choose the appropriate matrix format (L. T, X, Y shaped).

3. Draw the matrix.

4. List the items in each group along the axis of the matrix.

5. Decide what information you want to show with the symbols(numbers can be used to rank the relationship) on the matrix.

6. Compare groups. Item by item. Mark the appropriate symbol in the box at the intersection of the two items.

7. Complete the matrix with a legend describing the symbols.

8. Analyze the matrix for patterns.

Run Chart

A run chart is a graph that shows a measurement (vertical axis) against time (on the horizontal axis), with a reference line to show the average of the data.

Used when:

- During data collection, before enough points have been collected to draw a control chart

- Looking for trends or changes in the average

- Looking for cycles or other patterns

Process:

1. Decide on the vertical scale, based on the range of measurements you expect to see. Decide on the horizontal time scale, based on the frequency of measurements. Mark and label the scales.

2. If you already have historical data, calculate the average. Draw across the chart a reference line showing the average.

3. Plot each measurement in the time order it occurs. Connect points with straight lines.

4. Look for patterns in the data.

Index

root cause, 9, 53, 55

run chart, 71

S

Seven Step Problem Solving Model, 55

SIPOC chart, 29

sundial, 34

supplier, 13, 15, 36, 39, 40, 50, 53, 64, 65, 66

Supplier Requirements Table, 66

T

translate, 44

V

vital few, 25, 29, 30, 34, 49

vital few customers, 34

W

waste, 14

www.ingramcontent.com/pod-product-compliance
Lightning Source LLC
Chambersburg PA
CBHW060148200526
45165CB00023B/1331

* 9 7 8 1 4 3 9 2 0 1 0 4 6 *